A *LifeBuilder*

G000113876

SONGs *from* SCRIPTURE

9 studies
for individuals or groups

James W Reapsome

With Notes for Leaders

Scripture Union is an international Christian charity working with churches in more than 130 countries.

Thank you for purchasing this book. Any profits from this book support SU in England and Wales to bring the good news of Jesus Christ to children, young people and families and to enable them to meet God through the Bible and prayer.

Find out more about our work and how you can get involved at:

www.scriptureunion.org.uk (England and Wales)
www.suscotland.org.uk (Scotland)
www.suni.co.uk (Northern Ireland)
www.scriptureunion.org (USA)
www.su.org.au (Australia)

ISBN 978 1 78506 552 1

First published in the United States by InterVarsity Press 2016.
© James W Reapsome

Published in the United Kingdom © Scripture Union 2017.

British Library Cataloguing-in-Publication data: a catalogue record for this book is available from the British Library.

Printed in India by Thomson Press India Ltd

Image credit: mladn61/iStock by Getty Images

Contents

Getting the Most Out of *Songs from Scripture*

To get the most out of *Songs from Scripture*, imagine yourself in the audience listening to the climactic choral segment of Beethoven's Ninth Symphony. As you study these biblical songs, imagine how the music would sound if written to match the theme of the lyrics. These themes have not been set to music, but they come down to us as powerful expressions of personal faith at critical junctures in the story line of the Bible from creation to redemption.

"Sing praises to God, sing praises; / sing praises to our King, sing praises. / For God is the King of all the earth; / sing to him a psalm of praise" (Psalm 47:6-7). Songs lift our hearts and minds. They powerfully convey truth poetically and musically. God commands us to love him totally and exclusively with the union of our emotion, intellect and will. That's why he included songs when he inspired the words of the Bible.

Some biblical songs are lyrical, and they fit our desire for the symmetry of words and music. The psalms, for example, fit admirably as hymns, even today. But the Bible's songs also include stunningly simple and classic summaries of foundational truth.

Genesis 1, for example, was not composed to be set to music, but in the larger sense the majesty, beauty and power of the creation story have served to inspire countless songs of praise.

Because songs were the major means of teaching and transmitting God's truth in earlier centuries, the New Testament writers did not teach truth in poetry to the same degree we find in the Old Testament. Nevertheless, apart from straight narratives, songs in the broadest sense illuminate the pages of the Gospels, Epistles and Revelation. Apostolic declarations constituted the early church's repertoire of songs.

Hebrew poetry does not fit the literary formats of historic English poetry. Worshipers of the God who inspired the Old Testament are therefore required to do more thoughtful reflection than usual. But to be quiet before God and meditate on his songs brings immense spiritual dividends.

This work is not a textbook about or guide to biblical poetry. It is intended to spark communion with God through our emotions, making for truly inspiring worship. Biblical songs inspire both meditation and celebration. This study guide is intended to call God's people to find eternal truth in new and fresh ways so their worship experiences are more satisfying personally and more pleasing to God.

Suggestions for Individual Study

1. As you begin each study, pray that God will speak to you through his Word.

2. Read the introduction to the study and respond to the personal reflection question or exercise. This is designed to help you focus on God and on the theme of the study.

3. Each study deals with a particular passage so that you can delve into the author's meaning in that context. Read and reread the passage to be studied. The questions are written using the language of the New International Version, so you may wish to use that version of the Bible. The New Revised Standard Version is also recommended.

4. This is an inductive Bible study, designed to help you discover for yourself what Scripture is saying. The study includes three types of questions. Observation questions ask about the basic facts: who, what, when, where and how. Interpretation questions delve into the meaning of the passage. Application questions help you discover the implications of the text for growing in Christ. These three keys unlock the treasures of Scripture.

Write your answers to the questions in the spaces provided or in a personal journal. Writing can bring clarity and deeper understanding of yourself and of God's Word.

5. It might be good to have a Bible dictionary handy. Use it to look up any unfamiliar words, names or places.

6. Use the prayer suggestion to guide you in thanking God for what you have learned and to pray about the applications that have come to mind.

7. You may want to go on to the suggestion under "Now or Later," or you may want to use that idea for your next study.

Suggestions for Members of a Group Study

1. Come to the study prepared. Follow the suggestions for individual study mentioned above. You will find that careful preparation will greatly enrich your time spent in group discussion.

2. Be willing to participate in the discussion. The leader of your group will not be lecturing. Instead, he or she will be encouraging the members of the group to discuss what they have learned. The leader will be asking the questions that are found in this guide.

3. Stick to the topic being discussed. Your answers should be based on the verses that are the focus of the discussion and not on outside authorities such as commentaries or speakers. These studies focus on a particular passage of Scripture. Only rarely should you refer to other portions of the Bible. This allows for everyone to participate in in-depth study on equal ground.

4. Be sensitive to the other members of the group. Listen attentively when they describe what they have learned. You may be surprised by their insights! Each question assumes a variety of answers. Many questions do not have "right" answers, particularly questions that aim at meaning or application. Instead the questions push us to explore the passage more thoroughly.

When possible, link what you say to the comments of others. Also, be affirming whenever you can. This will encourage some of the more hesitant members of the group to participate.

5. Be careful not to dominate the discussion. We are sometimes so eager to express our thoughts that we leave too little opportunity for others to respond. By all means participate! But allow others to also.

6. Expect God to teach you through the passage being discussed and through the other members of the group. Pray that you will have an enjoyable and profitable time together, but also that as a result of the study you will find ways that you can take action individually and/or as a group.

7. Remember that anything said in the group is considered confidential and should not be discussed outside the group unless specific permission is given to do so.

8. If you are the group leader, you will find additional suggestions at the back of the guide.

1

Song of Creation

For the first time, a litter of four infant star siblings have been seen gestating in the belly of a gas cloud. Researchers say the finding supports the theory that most stars do not begin their lives alone. In the Perseus star-forming region, four stars are emerging from a single parent filament, and have been observed moving together as a family. Three of the siblings are balls of gas (within the larger gas filament) that researchers say are on the cusp of collapsing into stars, while the fourth sibling has already become a star.

Scientists estimate that more than half of all stars like our sun live with a partner star, and yet scientists have little observational evidence to suggest whether these stars are born together, like twins, or come together later in life. Double-star systems affect many areas of astronomy, including the search for black holes and for habitable exoplanets. The new findings could give scientists a better idea of how multistar systems emerge.

GROUP DISCUSSION. On a regular basis we learn about some new, mind-stretching aspect of creation. How do you respond to these kinds of discoveries?

PERSONAL REFLECTION. Think about the last time you sensed God's presence as you marveled at something in creation. What made this experience possible for you?

Psalm 8 is one of several songs celebrating God as Creator. The singers accepted that the observable world around them —earth, skies and seas—was the handiwork of God who was therefore owed praise and obedience. They found in him the security they needed when facing overwhelming enemies of one kind or another. *Read Psalm 8.*

---

1. In your own words, what are the song's major themes and goals?

---

2. What is wrapped up in the confession "our Lord"?

---

3. How does your personal relationship with God affect the way you look at creation?

---

4. As you reflect on God's majesty in creation, what thoughts, ideas and questions occur to you?

5. In what ways does your response compare to the singers'?

6. How would you answer the song's question in verse 4?

7. How have you experienced God's care?

How do you respond to his care?

8. What difference does it make that you are "crowned . . . with glory and honor" (v. 5)?

9. What responsibilities has God given to humans (vv. 6-8)?

In what ways do you, or could you, fulfill these responsibilities?

10. How does this song help you praise God?

How does it help you apply God's power and love to your needs for faith, hope and courage?

Ask God to make you sensitive to his power, love and wisdom in the world around you. Pray that you will not allow the world's noise to keep you from thanking and praising his majesty and name in all the earth.

Now or Later

Rehearse this creation song in your mind and compose a song of your own. Keep your main points simple so you can comfortably and wisely share them as part of your Christian witness. For example, consider how song writers ancient and modern have rephrased Psalm 8.

2

Song of Deliverance

Few events in history have captured the imaginations of poets, writers and filmmakers like Israel's deliverance from slavery in Egypt. Called simply "the exodus," it has been the cornerstone of Jewish faith down through the centuries. At the same time, bondage to cruel despots has never been stamped out. People of every era and culture have cried to God for deliverance. Somehow, people seem to know there is a true, living God in heaven who cares about us.

GROUP DISCUSSION. What different forms of bondage and slavery exist today? What means of deliverance are offered to hurting people?

PERSONAL REFLECTION. Have you ever felt enslaved by something? How did deliverance come to you?

In poetic form, Exodus 15 thrills us to the core. We can imagine being one of the millions of Israelites who have just escaped slaughter by Pharaoh's fast-encroaching army, only to witness them drowning in the Red Sea. We have just set our feet on dry ground when Moses, our captain, breaks out in song. His song is a balm to our terrified spirits. *Read Exodus 15:1-21.*

1. What spirit and tone permeate this song?

2. Why might Moses have resorted to poetry and music instead of lecturing about what God had done?

3. How does Moses picture his relationship with God (v. 2)?

How do his metaphors give credibility and authenticity to his song?

4. How do you use songs to teach the basics of Christian truth in your church?

5. How do the graphic poetic details in this song (vv. 6-12) enhance Israel's estimation of God's wisdom and power?

6. As a consequence, how should the people respond to this kind of God (vv. 1-3, 6-7, 11-13, 18, 21)?

7. What does the song foretell about Israel's future (vv. 13, 17)?

How did these events fuel their faith to move ahead?

8. What milestone events in your life could you set to music?

9. Why is it essential to tell your life-changing events over and over again, whether set to music or not?

10. What is the essence of Miriam's song?

Why might she have instigated her own celebration with the women?

---

11. In what ways is this song about Israel's exodus from Egypt a picture of the Christian's deliverance from the power and bondage of sin?

Thank God that through the death and resurrection of Jesus we can be liberated from sin. Ask him each day for resurrection power to be delivered from saying yes to sin's temptations.

Now or Later

Since the exodus is such a popular theme in books and films, consider the possibility of inviting some friends to watch a movie and compare it to the biblical record. Suggest some ideas about how liberation is both personal and political. Be clear about a brief story of your own.

3

Song of Invitation

Invitations from God accompanied by promises and warnings pour out from the pages of Scripture. They reveal God's nature and our needs. We probably are most familiar with the story Jesus told about the wedding feast, an alarming picture of people who refused to accept the invitation (Matthew 22:1-14). Such is our perversity, yet God never quits inviting us to come to him for forgiveness, joy, peace and purpose. His invitations point us to the supreme value of knowing and serving the living God.

GROUP DISCUSSION. Describe the attractiveness of our culture's varied "invitations." What do they appeal to? Why?

PERSONAL REFLECTION. At what turning point in your life did God offer you an invitation? What steps to spiritual growth did his invitation draw you to? How did you respond? Why?

Isaiah's prophetic invitation foretells many similar calls in the New Testament. It was directed to God's people suffering in captivity in Babylon because of their past disobedience to the Lord. They were in chains, so to speak, but they could be liberated because God cared and offered them a new way of life. See how the song celebrates his love, which he gave freely, and his promise of relief, forgiveness and hope. *Read Isaiah 55.*

---

1. What various commands does the prophet use in his song of invitation (vv. 1-3, 6-7)?

---

2. What promises does this song give to those who accept the invitation?

---

3. What does God invite you to?

How would you picture your appropriate responses?

---

4. To what high point in Israel's history does the song testify (vv. 4-5)?

5. What facts do we learn about God in the last stanza (vv. 8-13)?

What does God promise?

6. How do these promises differ from those in the first stanza and encourage one to accept God's invitation?

7. Why are these truths needed to provide strong support for the invitations?

8. How does the indictment of verses 8-9 fit the overall tone and spirit of this song?

Is it really necessary? Why or why not?

9. As you worship in song, how do you include both your personal feelings toward God and what you know to be true about him?

10. How do the poetic pictures of verses 10-13 speak to your personal needs in worship?

---

11. If you were captive in Babylon, how would you feel after singing this song? Why?

Ask God to make you sensitive to his patient, loving calls to fellowship, worship and service. Pray for wisdom and courage to reject the world's invitations to material satisfaction.

Now or Later

Invite a friend to meet you for coffee or a sandwich. Plan to share a brief story about some significant way you have chosen to follow the Lord because you have realized the kind of life he offers you. Use some metaphors of your own or borrow Isaiah's.

4

Song of Hope

Jeremiah 31:1-14, 31-34

Throughout history songs of hope have served to ameliorate the suffering of captive peoples. For example, the songs known as Negro spirituals—sung by thousands of slaves in America—are remembered and sung today. Because exile and captivity fell upon the Israelites, the Hebrew prophets of the Old Testament used poetry to teach both judgment and redemption. Their songs conveyed truth with power and passion. Since those days, hope has been the consistent theme of Scripture from the Old Testament through the culmination of history in the book of Revelation.

GROUP DISCUSSION. Why is hope such a critical component of spiritual and psychological health? In what ways is Christian hope substantially different from generic hope?

PERSONAL REFLECTION. What songs of hope have lifted your spirits? Why were the lyrics so personally applicable to your situation and feelings? Recall some of those words and phrases.

Some scholars think that Jeremiah's nickname, "the weep-ing prophet," is an unfair summary of his life. He was deeply touched by the impending doom of God's judgment on his people, but he also showed remarkable resilience and faith, as well as hope, in the long run. Because his prophecy is not re-corded chronologically, it's hard to follow his story. Judgment for rampant sin is Jeremiah's major theme, but light and hope penetrate the darkness in his songs as well. Set in the dark and final days of Israel's existence as a national entity, Jeremiah's song offers hope for better days to come in chapters 30–33. *Read Jeremiah 31:1-6.*

---

1. How does the general theme of this stanza offer hope to God's people?

---

2. What does this theme reveal about God and his relationship with his people?

---

3. If you were creating a painting of verses 1-6, what scenes would you include?

---

4. What metaphors can you use to describe God's everlasting love in your life?

5. In what circumstances have you felt a unique need to be assured of God's everlasting love?

Read Jeremiah 31:7-14.

6. What reasons does the singer give in verses 8-14 for his two commands in verse 7?

7. If you had been among the captives in exile in Babylon, what psychological or emotional effects would this stanza have had on you?

8. What reasons do you have for rejoicing "in the bounty of the LORD" (v. 12)?

Read Jeremiah 31:31-34.

9. What main points does the singer make in verses 31-32 to introduce the theme of this stanza?

10. How would you define God's new covenant in your own words?

_____

11. How does this stanza of the song give hope and courage to the exiles?

What would be required of them in response?

_____

12. How do you celebrate God's covenant of grace that gives you forgiveness and eternal life?

How does this song influence your worship?

Thank God for giving you hope through his wise and loving desire to have a covenant relationship with you in Jesus Christ.

Now or Later

Consider the covenants (mutual agreements) you now live with. Plan some specific activities that will show the priority your covenant with God has in your life. Write a descriptive verse about it.

5

Song of Despair

Despair is not a word that zips across the social media circuits. We use words like *oppression*, *persecution* or *exploitation* to picture very painful, often unjust, circumstances for which there is no relief in sight. But if we were to visit Nigeria, for example, and talk to the people who have lost their homes and families to marauding gangs, they would say they are overcome by despair. Despair includes distress and trouble of all kinds, not just physical suffering but also extreme emotional and spiritual stress caused by both external and internal pressures. Despair is very much a universal malady even though the word may have disappeared from our everyday usage.

GROUP DISCUSSION. What examples of social or personal despair come to mind? What harmful outcomes do people face under these circumstances? What successful relief attempts can you cite?

PERSONAL REFLECTION. Jesus said his followers could expect serious trouble, but he told them not to despair (John 16:33). In what circumstances have you felt unusual pressure and stress?

Job's saga begins with the catastrophic loss of all of his property, possessions and family. Three friends arrive to comfort and console Job, but they only add to his misery by blaming him for all that has befallen him. Job rises to defend himself and his character, but his friends remain unmoved. Chapter 19 is Job's sixth reply to his friends' charges. *Read Job 19:1-12, 21-27.*

---

1. How did Job's misguided friends add to his despair?

---

2. Why do the words of well-meaning friends so often bring judgment rather than encouragement?

How do you handle the subsequent distress?

---

3. What does Job accuse God of (v. 6)?

---

4. What feelings of despair does Job blame God for?

5. Which hardship do you think was the most difficult for Job to endure? Why?

6. Put Job's dramatic lyrics into your own words and tell which cause of his despair you most closely identify with.

7. When you feel you have been wronged, and as the aggrieved person you get no response, help or justice, what do you tell God?

8. Describe Job's vision for the future in your own words (vv. 23-27).

9. How did Job's vision lift him from the depths of despair to triumphant hope?

10. Compare Job's heart yearning for God (v. 27) with the various steps people take today in their efforts to ease the pain of their despair.

---

11. How do your mood changes follow the pattern of Job's song?

What does this tell you about the life of obedient faith in Christ?

Ask God for courage, faith and hope when you encounter distress and trouble that leads to despair. Pray for patient endurance while you look for answers. Pray with thanksgiving for what you know is good, right and true. Ask friends to pray with you.

Now or Later

After reflecting on Job's compelling song, compose something similar after you have come through a time of despair.

6

Song of Triumph

Scenes of triumph remain indelibly impressed on the minds and hearts of those who witnessed the wild, chaotic celebrations that marked the end of World War II in 1945. Suddenly, the release of pent-up emotions exploded everywhere. The war was over; victory was ours at last.

God's people have long been called to claim victory and triumph because the very heart of their faith rests on a triumphant God. "Faith is the victory that overcomes the world" has been their battle cry, despite tears of tragic losses and suffering. Somehow, out of the pits of darkness Christians have declared, "Yes, we look like losers, but we are the true winners. You may torture and kill us, but we will not die. We are triumphant because Jesus, our King, reigns on high."

To be triumphant is not to be cocky but to be confident in God's transcendent power and glory. Mary the mother of Jesus grew up in her country's weakness and despair, but her faith catapulted her to triumph.

GROUP DISCUSSION. As you look at the church's history, when was it right or wrong to act triumphantly in the world? Why? How have Christians behaved when they have lost everything?

PERSONAL REFLECTION. When have you needed a good dose of celebrating your triumphs by faith? How did you move from darkness to light?

Mary's song of triumph (the *Magnificat*, Latin for "my soul magnifies") is perhaps the most celebrated of the biblical songs because it exhibits such joyous, powerful faith by an unheralded teenage Jewish girl living in bondage to a foreign power. The immediate cause of her outburst of celebration was the angel Gabriel's announcement that she had been chosen by the Lord to bear a son who would rule an everlasting kingdom. In the face of seeming impossibility Mary had submitted to being the Lord's obedient servant (Luke 1:26-38). She rushed off to see her relative Elizabeth and tell her the startling news. After Elizabeth called her "blessed" (Luke 1:39-45), Mary broke into song. *Read Luke 1:46-55.*

1. Dissect Mary's preamble (vv. 46-49). What do you learn about her spiritual and physical circumstances?

What does she give God the credit for?

2. Why was her confession an appropriate way to begin her song of triumph?

3. What impresses you about Mary's knowledge of God as a teenage girl?

4. In your discoveries about God, how have you grown in your understanding of his grace, love and power?

5. Why did Mary believe that future generations would honor and bless her?

6. In our Christian songs of triumph, how can we match Mary's humility and her understanding of who God is and what he is like?

7. Look at the specific deeds Mary chose to illustrate God's triumphs (vv. 50-55). Why do you think she sang about these particular deeds?

8. Powerful lyrics arise from vivid contrasts. Identify the contrasts in Mary's song (vv. 51-53). What do they add to her sense of victory?

9. How did God's victories become a source of triumph for Mary?

---

10. What does Mary's choice of things to celebrate teach us about pride and humility?

How does our pride sometimes spoil our victories?

---

11. Choose one word that best summarizes this young girl's religious understanding and faith. Which of her attributes would you like to develop in yourself?

Ask God to fill you with joy and praise in the midst of even your darkest circumstances. Pray that you will experience the triumph that comes from your obedient faith.

Now or Later

You are writing your song of triumph. How would it go? What would you include? Why?

7

Song of Humility

Philippians 2:5-11

Nothing offends God as much as human pride. The Tower of Babel pierced the sky as a monument to pride so God destroyed it. Other ancient kings also paid dearly for taking credit for their achievements. Egypt's Pharaoh rejected orders from God through Moses, and his pride brought his realm untold misery and disaster. But object lessons from history fail to dent popular culture, which is obsessed with the pride of being the best at everything. For many people humility doesn't register on their list of personal goals. It's assumed that being humble means being willing to be stepped on. Who needs that?

GROUP DISCUSSION. What powers in popular culture seem to ridicule humble persons? Why do entertainment and sports personalities seem to feed on their pride? How does pride affect issues between nations? Religious differences?

PERSONAL REFLECTION. Think of someone's humility and how it touched you. Think of someone's pride and how it offended you. What made the difference?

Typically, Paul's correspondence teaches doctrine and then reveals how the doctrine forms the basis of a completely new and revolutionary life style. His letter to the Philippians does not exactly follow that pattern. Seemingly, from out of nowhere he expounds the two natures of Christ in the context of humility. *Read Philippians 2:5-11.*

1. In what context does the apostle Paul offer this song of humility (vv. 1-4)?

2. Why do you suppose this was such a crucial issue to him?

3. If you were to choose one aspect of your Christian character to write about, would it be humility? Why or why not?

4. What basic command does Paul give (v. 5)?

Why is that such a tall order?

5. List the examples of Christ's humility (vv. 6-8).

In Paul's mind, what was the climactic event on which to focus his theme?

---

6. How does the cross smash human pride and give us an example of how to live?

---

7. The key, tempo and volume of a piece of music help us to understand it. If Paul's song were set to music, how would you contrast verses 9-11 with verses 6-8?

---

8. What is the universal scope of God's plan for his Son (vv. 9-11)?

---

9. What is the connection between Christ's past humiliation and his future exaltation?

10. In a world that celebrates pride and ridicules the name of Jesus, how do Christians humbly affirm the supremacy of the name of Jesus?

What does his name represent to you?

Thank and praise God for the incomparable humbling of his Son so we might be absolved of our sins and enter his kingdom. Ask that the power of his humility might transform your life.

Now or Later

Make a checklist with two columns: first, situations when your pride took charge; second, situations when your humility triumphed. Ask what made the difference and why.

8

Song of Glory

Perhaps the apostle Paul's song of glory for Christians was inspired by a scene he had witnessed in Rome (2 Corinthians 2:14; Colossians 2:15). Romans publicly celebrated the success of military commanders who led their forces to victory in the service of the state. On the day of his triumph, the general wore a crown of laurel and the gold-embroidered purple triumphal toga, regalia that identified him as nearly divine or nearly a king. He rode in a four-horse chariot through the streets of Rome in unarmed procession with his army, captives and the spoils of his war. To Paul, this must have seemed like small potatoes compared to the glory of almighty God, whom he loved, served and worshiped.

Since then, Christians have tried to glorify God with their art, architecture and music. Gothic cathedrals are one example; Crusader forts are another. I trudged through an enormous Crusader fort in Kerak, Jordan, part of a chain of fortresses that led to Jerusalem. The builders said they mounted huge blocks of stone to glorify God. The sight gave me pause to ask myself, *How do I glorify God?* It's a matter of heart, mind and will that will not go away.

GROUP DISCUSSION. What different forms of Christian worship have stirred you to glorify God? Why? Why is this basic Christian concept so hard for us to sink our teeth into?

PERSONAL REFLECTION. What does it mean to you to claim that everything you do is for God's glory? How does that goal shape your daily routine?

Paul's song in Romans 11:33-36 seems like the sudden appearance of a brilliant star breaking though clouds of uncertainty. Many difficult teachings in Romans 9–11 arise from Paul's treatise on the future of his own people, the Jews. Paul did not shrink from saying that God has not given up on the Jews, but that the failure of the Jews had opened the door to salvation for Gentiles. Somehow, the enormous magnitude of his teaching overwhelmed his soul. In spite of our feeble attempts to understand God's mind and purposes, he calls us to sing our unqualified praise of his glory (See Ephesians 1:6, 12, 14). God's glory overrides everything else. *Read Romans 11:33-36.*

1. What was Paul's understanding of God in this passage?

2. In what terms does he establish God's supremacy?

3. In light of the sticky theological problems Paul was dealing with (Romans 9–11), why was it good medicine to sing this doxology?

---

4. How has singing your faith helped you to dispel the clouds in your soul?

---

5. What do you do when you find it hard to figure out what God is up to?

---

6. If the depths and riches of God are beyond our understanding, why and how can we glorify God?

---

7. What are some examples of the "all things" (v. 36) that come from God and return to God?

8. By implication, this song of praise includes a warning (vv. 34-35). How would you describe these perils?

How can you avoid them?

---

9. "To him be the glory" (v. 36) is a tall order. What does that mean and how do you carry it out?

---

10. In your congregational setting, how do you affirm your faith in song?

How do you keep your focus on God's eternal glory rather than your emotional feelings?

Ask God to allow your heart and mind to focus on him as you read Scripture and pray. Ask him to close your mind to your own problems for a minute or two at least.

Now or Later

Make a search of biblical songs, blessings or benedictions. Store them in a separate document in your computer files. Refer to them for yourself, or email to others who send you some news for prayer.

9

Song of Redemption

Redemption (and its cognates) has slipped from our religious vocabulary. The New International Version of the Bible has replaced it with *purchased* (Revelation 5:9), which hardly packs the same wallop. I grew up singing the power-laden strains of "Redeemed, how I love to proclaim it. Redeemed by the blood of the Lamb" ringing in my ears and heart. Part of the demise of *redeemed* can be attributed to the fact that many people have never heard of the idea that we are bound in slavery to selfishness and pride and must therefore be set free. In other words, we must be purchased or *redeemed* to gain our freedom. If we could speak with slaves, we would understand very well what it means to be redeemed.

GROUP DISCUSSION. How does the goal of attaining eternal bliss in heaven affect people you know? Why has joining the hosts of heaven in singing praises to Jesus Christ lost its luster as an eternal destiny? How can it be regained?

PERSONAL REFLECTION. How do you maintain a heart for what you know lies ahead in heavenly worship? What values does this perspective enhance in your life? If you asked God to make you fit for heaven, what would change in your life? Why?

The book of Revelation scares off people because of its mystery-laden battles between good and evil. But before the powers of darkness are unleashed Jesus speaks to seven congregations (chaps. 1–3). Then the glorious throne and magnificent worship in heaven come into view, followed by the coronation of Jesus as the Lamb who will rule the world. Worship suffuses chapters 4–5 before the cosmic struggles begin. We get glimpses of spectacular scenes of worship again in chapters 7 and 11. *Read Revelation 5:6-14.*

---

1. If you were producing a television documentary about heaven based on this song, how would you identify and describe what you wanted to highlight and focus on?

---

2. What are the distinguishing marks and roles of the Lamb, the creatures, the elders, the angels and "every creature"?

---

3. In what sense is this song a song of redemption?

Who is redeemed?

By whom and at what cost?

4. What does it mean to you to be redeemed, or purchased, by the blood of the Lamb?

What difference does it make in your life?

5. How does a worship scene like this touch you intellectually and emotionally?

6. How do you explain the apparently contradictory visions of the Lamb: first slain, then given power, glory and honor?

7. Why is the imagery and metaphor of the Lamb so powerful?

What does it add to the spirit of worship in the song?

8. If you played a part in this scene of your documentary, what would it be and why?

---

9. How does this song enhance and inspire your anticipation of heaven?

---

10. Notice the widening circle and scope of singers who honor the Lamb (vv. 8-9, 11-12, 13). What does this say to you about the universal, everlasting power of the gospel of the crucified Christ and your place in spreading the song of redemption?

Ask God for a positive, worshipful approach to Revelation. Thank him for revealing scenes of glory, praise, majesty and honor regarding Jesus the Lamb of God who gave his life for us.

Now or Later

Look up some classical paintings of this scene on the Internet. (For example, *Adoration of the Lamb* by Jan van Eyck [1432]). What do they emphasize? How would you paint this scene?

Leader's Notes

MY GRACE IS SUFFICIENT FOR YOU. (2 COR 12:9)

Leading a Bible discussion can be an enjoyable and rewarding experience. But it can also be *scary*—especially if you've never done it before. If this is your feeling, you're in good company. When God asked Moses to lead the Israelites out of Egypt, he replied, "O Lord, please send someone else to do it!" (Ex 4:13). It was the same with Solomon, Jeremiah and Timothy, but God helped these people in spite of their weaknesses, and he will help you as well.

You don't need to be an expert on the Bible or a trained teacher to lead a Bible discussion. The idea behind these inductive studies is that the leader guides group members to discover for themselves what the Bible has to say. This method of learning will allow group members to remember much more of what is said than a lecture would.

These studies are designed to be led easily. As a matter of fact, the flow of questions through the passage from observation to interpretation to application is so natural that you may feel that the studies lead themselves. This study guide is also flexible. You can use it with a variety of groups—student, professional, neighborhood or church groups. Each study takes forty-five to sixty minutes in a group setting.

There are some important facts to know about group dynamics and encouraging discussion. The suggestions listed below should enable you to effectively and enjoyably fulfill your role as leader.

Preparing for the Study

1. Ask God to help you understand and apply the passage in your own life. Unless this happens, you will not be prepared to lead others. Pray too for the various members of the group. Ask God to open your hearts to the message of his Word and motivate you to action.

2. Read the introduction to the entire guide to get an overview of the entire book and the issues that will be explored.

3. As you begin each study, read and reread the assigned Bible passage to familiarize yourself with it.

4. This study guide is based on the New International Version of the Bible. It will help you and the group if you use this translation as the basis for your study and discussion.

5. Carefully work through each question in the study. Spend time in meditation and reflection as you consider how to respond.

6. Write your thoughts and responses in the space provided in the study guide. This will help you to express your understanding of the passage clearly.

7. It might help to have a Bible dictionary handy. Use it to look up any unfamiliar words, names or places. (For additional help on how to study a passage, see chapter five of *How to Lead a LifeGuide Bible Study*, InterVarsity Press.)

8. Consider how you can apply the Scripture to your life. Remember that the group will follow your lead in responding to the studies. They will not go any deeper than you do.

9. Once you have finished your own study of the passage, familiarize yourself with the leader's notes for the study you are leading. These are designed to help you in several ways. First, they tell you the purpose the study guide author had in mind when writing the study. Take time to think through how the study questions work together to accomplish that purpose. Second, the notes provide you with additional background information or suggestions on group dynamics for various questions. This information can be useful when people have difficulty understanding or answering a question. Third, the leader's notes can alert you to potential problems you may encounter during the study.

10. If you wish to remind yourself of anything mentioned in the leader's notes, make a note to yourself below that question in the study.

Leading the Study

1. Begin the study on time. Open with prayer, asking God to help the group to understand and apply the passage.

2. Be sure that everyone in your group has a study guide. Encourage the group to prepare beforehand for each discussion by reading the introduction to the guide and by working through the questions in the study.

3. At the beginning of your first time together, explain that these studies are meant to be discussions, not lectures. Encourage the members of the group to participate. However, do not put pressure on those who may be hesitant to speak during the first few sessions. You may want to suggest the following guidelines to your group.

☐ Stick to the topic being discussed.

☐ Your responses should be based on the verses that are the focus of the discussion and not on outside authorities such as commentaries or speakers.

☐ These studies focus on a particular passage of Scripture. Only rarely should you refer to other portions of the Bible. This allows for everyone to participate in in-depth study on equal ground.

☐ Anything said in the group is considered confidential and will not be discussed outside the group unless specific permission is given to do so.

☐ We will listen attentively to each other and provide time for each person present to talk.

☐ We will pray for each other.

4. Have a group member read the introduction at the beginning of the discussion.

5. Every session begins with a group discussion question. The question or activity is meant to be used before the passage is read. The question introduces the theme of the study and encourages group members to begin to open up. Encourage as many members as possible to participate, and be ready to get the discussion going with your own response.

This section is designed to reveal where our thoughts or feelings need to be transformed by Scripture. That is why it is especially important not to read the passage before the discussion question is asked. The passage will tend to color the honest reactions people would otherwise give because they are, of course, supposed to think the way the Bible does.

You may want to supplement the group discussion question with an icebreaker to help people to get comfortable. See the community section of *Small Group Idea Book* for more ideas.

You also might want to use the personal reflection question with your group. Either allow a time of silence for people to respond individually or discuss it together.

6. Have a group member (or members if the passage is long) read aloud the passage to be studied. Then give people several minutes to read the passage again silently so that they can take it all in.

7. Question 1 will generally be an overview question designed to briefly survey the passage. Encourage the group to look at the whole passage, but try to avoid getting sidetracked by questions or issues that will be addressed later in the study.

8. As you ask the questions, keep in mind that they are designed to be used just as they are written. You may simply read them aloud. Or you may prefer to express them in your own words.

There may be times when it is appropriate to deviate from the study guide. For example, a question may have already been answered. If so, move on to the next question. Or someone may raise an important question not covered in the guide. Take time to discuss it, but try to keep the group from going off on tangents.

9. Avoid answering your own questions. If necessary, repeat or rephrase them until they are clearly understood. Or point out something you read in the leader's notes to clarify the context or meaning. An eager group quickly becomes passive and silent if they think the leader will do most of the talking.

10. Don't be afraid of silence. People may need time to think about the question before formulating their answers.

11. Don't be content with just one answer. Ask, "What do the rest of you think?" or "Anything else?" until several people have given answers to the question.

12. Acknowledge all contributions. Try to be affirming whenever possible. Never reject an answer. If it is clearly off-base, ask, "Which verse led you to that conclusion?" or again, "What do the rest of you think?"

13. Don't expect every answer to be addressed to you, even though this will probably happen at first. As group members become more at ease, they will begin to truly interact with each other. This is one sign of healthy discussion.

14. Don't be afraid of controversy. It can be very stimulating. If you don't resolve an issue completely, don't be frustrated. Move on and keep it in mind for later. A subsequent study may solve the problem.

15. Periodically summarize what the group has said about the passage. This helps to draw together the various ideas mentioned and gives continuity to the study. But don't preach.

16. At the end of the Bible discussion you may want to allow group members a time of quiet to work on an idea under "Now or Later." Then discuss what you experienced. Or you may want to encourage group members to work on these ideas between meetings. Give an opportunity during the session for people to talk about what they are learning.

17. Conclude your time together with conversational prayer, adapting the prayer suggestion at the end of the study to your group. Ask for God's help in following through on the commitments you've made.

18. End on time.

Many more suggestions and helps are found in *How to Lead a LifeGuide Bible Study.*

Components of Small Groups

A healthy small group should do more than study the Bible. There are four components to consider as you structure your time together.

Nurture. Small groups help us to grow in our knowledge and love of God. Bible study is the key to making this happen and is the foundation of your small group.

Community. Small groups are a great place to develop deep friendships with other Christians. Allow time for informal interaction before and after each study. Plan activities and games that will help you get to know each other. Spend time having fun together going on a picnic or cooking dinner together.

Worship and prayer. Your study will be enhanced by spending time praising God together in prayer or song. Pray for each other's needs and keep track of how God is answering prayer in your group. Ask God to help you to apply what you are learning in your study.

Outreach. Reaching out to others can be a practical way of applying what you are learning, and it will keep your group from becoming self-focused. Host a series of evangelistic discussions for your friends or neighbors. Clean up the yard of an elderly friend. Serve at a soup kitchen together or spend a day working on a Habitat house.

Many more suggestions and helps in each of these areas are found in *Small Group Idea Book*. Information on building a small group can be found in *Small Group Leaders' Handbook* and *The Big Book on Small Groups* (both from InterVarsity Press). Reading through one of these books would be worth your time.

Study 1. Song of Creation. Psalm 8.

Purpose: To discover the majesty of God's work and name in creation, and to develop more significant patterns of worship arising from such discoveries.

Question 1. Psalm 8 is one of the songs of creation (see also Psalm 19; 104; 139) used on special days of celebration and worship. Although a song of creation, its lyrics do not simply praise nature. The poetry points us to God, who made everything. In the opening the singers are overwhelmed by the greatness and splendor of God. *Majestic* (or *excellent*) suggests splendor or magnificence.

"Name" is hard to get our heads around, although it is quite a significant biblical concept. "Name" did more than identify a person. It communicated something of the essence, character or reputation of the person. Names became especially significant when linked with truth about God. In this case, as in other psalms (e.g., Psalm 54:1, 6), God's name is the summation of his person and character.

Question 2. The singer uses the personal pronouns *our* and *your* for the first time in the Psalter to reinforce the truth of God's special relationship with his people. Thus he speaks for all those who gathered to worship the Lord.

Question 3. Help the group to be specific. Use an illustration of your own.

Question 6. The words for "mankind" emphasize their weakness in contrast to the vastness of the universe. They denote humans in their frailty, impotence and mortality. The literal meaning of *mindful* is remember; *care* means "to pay attention to."

Question 7. God's care is his constant, loving, providential work for our benefit.

Question 8. "Glory and honor" are divine attributes (see also Psalm 96:6) belonging to God himself. The New Testament points to Jesus in his present reign as the ultimate fulfillment (Ephesians 1:22). In this song, mankind is crowned king of creation.

Question 9. The singer is well versed in the teachings about creation in Genesis 1. Here he refers to Genesis 1:26, 28. The New Testament parallel is 1 Corinthians 15:27.

Study 2. Song of Deliverance. Exodus 15:1-21.

Purpose: To use this song as a pattern for personal reflection and celebration of God's strong deeds of salvation and growth in his love and grace.

Question 1. The Israelites' crossing of the Red Sea once more displayed the might and glory of God. It was the climax of the bitter struggle between Moses and Pharaoh for the freedom of the Hebrews after four hundred years of living in slavery under the Egyptians.

Question 2. The song switches from prose to poetry, which conveys better than prose the feelings of the Israelites as they worshiped the Lord. By reading what has already been recorded, we are encouraged to share the celebration.

Question 5. Verses 1-12 celebrate the overthrow of the Egyptians in the sea. Powerful poetic imagery is revealed in the fact that God's "right hand" is "majestic in power" (vv. 6, 12). Much later, King David prayed that God would show his great love because he saves by his right hand (Psalm 17:7). The song concludes by focusing on what God will do in the future, beyond the wilderness to the settlement in Canaan (vv. 13-18).

Question 6. Notice the core issue the Israelites grappled with then (v. 11) and throughout their history. This rhetorical question constituted the basic challenge of Israel's prophets from the days of Moses until the Babylonian captivity.

Question 7. This part of the song projects an astonishing revelation of Israel's life in the Promised Land of Canaan. Look for as many pictures as you can, playing the role of a travel guide. Note the different roles God will play in bringing about their new life. The picture of God's planting his people is picked up again in the song of Psalm 80:8, 15.

Question 10. Verse 21 probably records only the opening of Miriam's song, which repeats the start of Moses' song in verse 1.

Question 11. In the New Testament, Jesus accomplished by his death and resurrection what might be called the "final exodus"— that is, our full redemption from the judgment and power of sin (Romans 6:6-11). Christians are no longer slaves to sin.

Study 3. Song of Invitation. Isaiah 55.
Purpose: To find fulfillment and satisfaction by accepting God's grace freely offered to all.

Question 1. Isaiah's message to Israel's exiles (chaps. 40–55) includes both a strong appeal and an attractive promise. His metaphorical commands in verse 1 take us to street vendors who shout that their merchandise is free. "This call to the needy is unsurpassed for warmth of welcome, even in the NT" ("Isaiah," *New Bible Commentary*, ed. Gordon J. Wenham et al. [Downers Grove, IL: IVP Academic, 1994], 664).

Question 2. The basic promise in the historical setting is to leave Babylon's enticements ("what does not satisfy" [v. 2]), make the tough journey back to their home country and enjoy the land of God's blessings.

Question 3. Prepare a brief summary of Christ's invitations in the New Testament (e.g., Matthew 11:28; John 6:35; 7:37; Revelation 22:17). Verse 7 is a classic statement of repentance for both wicked deeds ("ways" or habits) and evil thoughts or plans. On the one hand, repentance is negative ("forsake"), while on the other it is also positive ("turn") and personal ("to the Lord").

Question 4. The exiles looked to a human deliverer like their great King David. Isaiah teaches them of their responsibility to carry out the purposes and functions of the king, both spiritually and earthly.

Question 5. Think of verses 8-13 as the song's last stanza. It differs in both tone and scope. Note that it does not include strong active verbs associated with the directives of verses 1-7. It majors more on promises.

Question 8. Verses 8-9 serve as the song's linchpin, connecting the commands of verses 6-7 with the promises of verses 10-13. Verses 8-9 "shame us out of our small expectations. God's thoughts are more far-reaching and more fertile, as well as higher, than ours" (ibid., 664).

Question 10. The song's refrain in verses 10-13 reaffirm the trustworthiness of God's promises. "The poetic language of the hymns of Israel can become a miraculous reality, when God reverses the effects of the Fall (cf. Gen. 3:17f.), to the blessings of man and his own glory" ("Isaiah," in *The International Bible Commentary*, ed. F. F. Bruce et al. [Grand Rapids: Zondervan, 1986], 758).

Study 4. Song of Hope. Jeremiah 31:1-14, 31-34.
Purpose: To gain confidence and hope in God's new covenant with his people.

Question 1. The interpretation of Old Testament prophecies is difficult when it comes to the long-term future. Many of them have been fulfilled, such as Israel's return from captivity in Babylon and the coming of Israel's Messiah. Regarding prophecies yet to be fulfilled, some interpreters think they will be fulfilled for God's ancient people Israel at some time in the future, while others think not, believing they have been fulfilled in the

church, not literally, but figuratively. The purpose of this study
is not to settle the matter one way or the other. Rather, this song
of hope will show us what it meant to God's people in exile in
Babylon and how it speaks to important themes in our lives.

The song speaks to "all the families of Israel," which includes
exiles from both the southern kingdom of Judah and the northern tribes of Israel (or Samaria) (v. 5).

Question 2. The Lord is the song leader here, and he grounds
his call for renewing his "favor" (v. 2) to those in exile because
his love is everlasting (v. 3). Consistently, throughout the Old
Testament, God is pictured as drawing his people to himself
through his "unfailing kindness" (v. 3).

Question 6. Both praise and prayer are called for (v. 7). Praise is
appropriate because God's promises are certain to be fulfilled.
At the same time, God sees prayer as the means of accomplishing his future purposes. Not even people most infirm and most
unfit for a long journey will be left behind (v. 8). Although they
will weep for their past sins, which brought about their captivity (v. 9), they will return with joy. God will provide water
to satisfy their thirst on their journey. No strong enemies will
prevent their successful return (v. 11).

In verses 15-22 the song focuses on both the hardships of
the captives and the promises of a better future. There is hope
for the future (v. 17). Jeremiah resumes prose in verses 23-30
to describe a dream he had of bountiful blessings to come. God
even reminds the prophet of his calling to uproot, build and
plant (cf. Jeremiah 1:10; 31:28).

Question 9. The third stanza of the song of hope celebrates
hope not just in terms of delivery from exile and a return to a
beautiful, rejuvenated land, but also in terms of a rejuvenated
people with new hearts and a profound understanding of what
it means to know and worship the Lord.

The Old Testament tells of various agreements, promises
or covenants between God and his people. For example, God

made special promises to Abraham and David. He gave laws to Moses that detailed the covenant, a binding agreement between two parties. Now, the song of hope speaks of a new plan for God's people based entirely on his grace and mercy. This was such a revolutionary idea that the New Testament addresses the subject by quoting Jeremiah 31:31-34 in Hebrews 8.

Study 5. Song of Despair. Job 19:1-12, 21-27.

Purpose: To learn from Job's experience how to move from despair to hope.

Question 1. Job's story begins with Satan's charge to God that Job was following God for personal gain. God allowed Satan to take everything except Job's life to prove his integrity. After intense suffering Job passed his test and three friends arrived to share his grief and lecture him. Two rounds of their speeches preceded Job's song in chapter 19, which is Job's sixth speech. The men kept hammering Job with the accepted wisdom of the day—that his suffering was caused by his sin.

Question 3. "God has wronged me" (v. 6) refers both to Job's undeserved suffering and to God's delay in clearing his name of any sin.

Question 4. Illustrating Job's despair, among other things, was his feeling that "there is no justice" (v. 7). Job did not accuse God of being unjust but rather that God was taking much too long to bring justice to Job's case.

Question 8. In verses 13-22 Job declares that God has alienated his friends and family from him. They regarded his disease as a sign of God's judgment.

"Inscribed with an iron tool" (v. 24) refers to the ancient practice of cutting an inscription into stone and then filling the letters with lead. Job demanded an indelible way of recording his words.

Consult various translations of verses 25-27. Compare and discuss the different words used for *redeemer*, such as *defender*.

Some interpreters see this as a picture of Jesus, the living Redeemer who came to earth and offered the godly participation in his resurrection. "Job is not necessarily thinking of a vindication beyond death, although his language by no means rules that out" ("Job," in *The International Bible Commentary*, ed. F. F. Bruce et al. [Grand Rapids: Zondervan, 1986], 533).

Briefly summarize the end of Job's spiritual journey out of despair from Job 42:1-6, after God had spoken to him (vv. 38-41). "My ears had heard of you but now my eyes have seen you" (Job 42:5). Job had repented.

Study 6. Song of Triumph. Luke 1:46-55.

Purpose: To discover appropriate formats for expressing the triumphs of God's grace, love and power, whether privately or in corporate worship.

Question 1. The preamble does not tell us all we would like to know about Mary. Focus on what she does reveal about herself. The best we can say is that she was a young woman, probably in her early teens, still a virgin, who lived in Nazareth and was engaged to be married to Joseph, a carpenter who traced his lineage to King David.

Question 3. Mary's hymn of triumph was a lyric poem steeped in Old Testament writings. Apparently she was very familiar with Hannah's song (1 Samuel 2:1-10), as well as with the psalms (e.g., Psalm 98:1; 138:6).

Often in the Old Testament God's "arm" would save his people. The principle that God exalts the humble and casts down the proud was common in the Old Testament. "Filling the hungry" comes from Psalm 107:9.

Question 7. Read between her lines. For example, "He has scattered those who are proud. . . . He has brought down rulers" likely refers to the end of Roman rule and oppression.

Question 8. "'This beautiful lyric . . . [is] an expression of personal emotions and experiences.' It is lyrical in tone not only because it is was what Wordsworth declared all lyric poetry to be—the 'spontaneous outflow of powerful feeling'—but also because Mary knew the OT thoroughly, and many portions, especially the lyrical ones, by heart. Their language became the natural vehicle of her praises" ("Luke," in *The International Bible Commentary*, ed. F. F. Bruce et al. [Grand Rapids: Zondervan, 1986], 1,189).

Question 11. Make a list of these words and contrast them with Mary's theme of triumph.

Study 7. Song of Humility. Philippians 2:5-11.

Purpose: To reflect on Christ's humility, confess pride and seek his empowerment to follow his example.

Question 1. Apparently Paul did not intend to write a theological treatise about Christ's two natures. The theology of his song was intended to deal with issues of pride in the church at Philippi. He saw humility among the Christians as a critical need. Later on he made one swift note of a dispute (Philippians 4:2-3).

Question 2. Throughout his letters Paul sought to build unity in the church (e.g., Philippians 1:27; 2:2; 2:14; Ephesians 5:21). Considering the varied backgrounds of his converts, this was a hard goal to attain.

Question 4. Personal attitudes are difficult to change, especially among older folks. Considering the prevailing values of Greek and Roman culture, it was seemingly impossible for Christians to change their deeply rooted attitudes. To make Christ the example looked like an impossible goal.

Question 6. The cross of Christ permeated Paul's living, teaching and writing. Christ crucified was the overarching theme of his life and of his evangelistic preaching (Galatians 2:20; 1 Corinthians 2:2).

Question 7. A key is the major or minor scale around which a piece of music revolves. A song in a major key is based on a major scale. A song in a minor key is based on a minor scale. For example, a composer uses the major key to convey feelings of positive emotions. The minor key conveys sadness or danger. **Question 8.** Note Paul's repetition of *every* (vv. 9-11). This song is one of the Bible's clearest visions of the future, with Christ at the center. Paul saw his vision as a powerful antidote to pagan idolatry and moral corruption.

Question 9. At first glance there appears to be no connection, because the world does not value humility. But this song captures the major thread of Scripture: out of suffering and humiliation comes the triumph of the spirit. The prophets foretold the Messiah's suffering before his glory. This theme has sustained martyrs and made them victors over their killers. Yes, Jesus suffered and died, but that is not the end of the story.

Study 8. Song of Glory. Romans 11:33-36.

Purpose: To join Paul's song of glory to God and allow your heart to be refreshed by the greatness of God's love, mercy and grace.

Question 1. Paul's letter to the Romans is an exquisite revelation of basic Christian doctrine. But there comes a point when he can't contain himself and he explodes with worship in the context of his overall teaching. For him, true theology must lead to worship, best expressed here in his magnificent doxology (see also 1 Timothy 1:17; 6:15-16).

Question 2. Paul sees God's lavish grace in terms of universal scope and blessing. Or, as we might say, from one end of the world to the other. Nothing escapes God's attention in accomplishing his eternal plan of salvation through Jesus Christ.

Question 3. The intensity of Paul's feelings about the future of the Jews, his people, demanded his extensive treatment of the subject (Romans 9–11). Therefore, he seems to release all his pent-up emotions in his song of glory, remarkably in very few words, without any apologies or explanations.

Question 4. For example, someone in the group might be able to tell how singing hymns at the memorial service for a loved one lifted their spirits.

Question 5. Figuring out God's ways is a constant theme of God's people in Scripture. Paul's song makes it clear that God's glory is the incomparable goal of everything, whether or not we get clear answers to our questions.

Question 6. There is a thundering crescendo here in Paul's song. Logically, of course, no human beings get inside God's mind. But Paul would not have us shut down our minds as we contemplate the greatness of our God. Instead, we keep on looking for ways to glorify him, even with our limited knowledge. Paul taught that Jesus is our wisdom (1 Corinthians 1:30). He asks, "'Who has known the mind of the Lord so as to instruct him?' But we have the mind of Christ" (1 Corinthians 2:16). We are "renewed in knowledge in the image of [our] Creator" (Colossians 3:10).

Question 7. Scripture declares the universal scope of God's reign, from the creation stories in Genesis to the climax of history in Revelation 4:11 and 5:12.

Question 8. Paul's song takes a dramatic turn here in the form of questions that reach the foundations of human experience. He does not cry out against willful disobedience to the Lord but against overweening pride and hypocrisy: the idea that God owes me something for what I've done for him. Verse 33 is all about God; verses 34-35 are about human beings who assume they know more than God does and who serve God for what they can get out of it. Some personal examples or stories would be helpful.

Question 9. *Glory* is an abstract idea to most people. We know what it is to glorify the stars who entertain us in sports, music and so on, but how does God's glory influence our everyday lives as well as our worship? Basically, it's all about who

God is—his character—and how he offers joy and peace in our knowledge of him. Songs like this one give us a pattern for glorifying God.

Study 9. Song of Redemption. Revelation 5:6-14.
Purpose: To gain a new perspective on heaven and heavenly worship.

Question 1. The immediate setting of John's heavenly vision of a sealed scroll produced a serious problem: Who could open the scroll? He was so upset that he wept and wept. Then one of the twenty-four elders (see Revelation 4:10) assured him that the Lion was able to do this. But instead of a Lion, John saw a Lamb, who was pronounced "worthy" to open the seven seals (cf. John 1:29, 36). Later in Revelation, "the Lamb" becomes the permanent title of Christ. Then the heavenly worship party erupted and John saw so much more than the Lamb. Each participant merits thoughtful meditation. As leader, keep the group moving.

Question 2. This song is packed with symbolism because of what seemed likely to be the annihilation of the church. Such apocalyptic symbolism was familiar to first-century Jews and Christians. Although different interpretations of the symbols abound, it is important to get the facts straight and not worry about having a uniform understanding of what they may or may not mean.

Question 3. Look up *redeemed* or *redemption* in a standard Bible dictionary. We could easily say that human redemption from the guilt, power and penalty of sin is the major thread of the entire biblical record. However, in contemporary thought and culture these concepts seem totally foreign. You might also discuss some synonyms and examples to show what sin encompasses.

Question 5. Biblical worship invariably includes the total person. It is never portrayed as a rote habit. In fact, Jesus warned against the perils of what he called worshiping in vain (Matthew 15:9). God's judgment on Israel was based on Israel's failure to love the one true God with heart, soul and strength (Deuteronomy 6:5).

Question 6. Keep in mind the immediate context of John's readers. How would the Lamb's life course be a preview of theirs?

Question 7. Lions fit the image of power and glory; lambs are gentle and weak. The juxtaposition of a lamb with power, wealth, wisdom, might, honor, glory and blessing catches our attention because it is so unusual.

Question 9. Try to recreate this song and list the changes it could bring to your life. John's vision was not given to provide a format for twenty-first-century Christian worship. It was set in the blood and thunder of the Roman Empire. Think of ways to use it to bring hope and comfort to people going through some difficult experiences.

Question 10. The sacrifice of the Lamb and his looming return as King of kings and Lord of lords have long been the lifeblood of the church in all cultures and under wicked, repressive governments. For example, Christians in Africa and Asia have developed distinctive ways to celebrate Christ's victory in times of intense persecution. (See Revelation 19:11-16 for the outcome of the Lamb's story.)

James Reapsome, a retired pastor, also formerly served as editor of Evangelical Missions Quarterly *and* World Pulse *newsletter as well as executive director of Evangelical Missions Information Service in Wheaton, Illinois.*

Scripture union

Have you ever asked yourself
How can I make a difference for God?

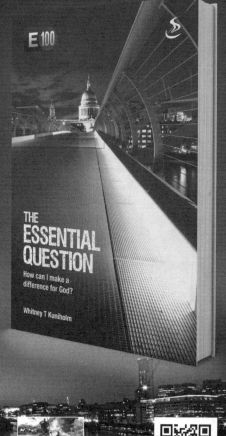

E 100

On some level, we all struggle to find our own answer to that fundamental question. The search for significance is the underlying motivation for virtually all human activity. It's what drives us.

The Essential Question takes you on a journey through the book of Acts. Fifty Bible readings to help you begin to find and follow God's plan for you today.

Single book:
978 1 84427 902 9
£6.99

5-pack also available:
978 1 84427 903 6
£25.00

THE
ESSENTIAL
QUESTION

How can I make a
difference for God?

Whitney T Kuniholm

ESSENTIAL 100

Single book:
978 1 84427 566 3
£6.99

5-pack also available:
978 1 84427 546 5
£25.00

ESSENTIAL JESUS

Single book:
978 184427 238 9
£6.99

5-pack also available:
978 184427 239 6
£25.00

Big Bible Challenge

Single book:
978 1 84427 584 7
£9.99

SCAN HERE
FOR MORE INFO

rder from your local Christian bookshop | Order from Scripture Union: 01908 856006 | Order online www.scriptureunion.org.uk

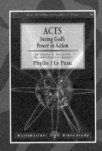
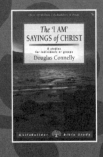